The Role of NLP in Overcoming Anxiety and Depression

By Rex Morton

Copyright Page

Published by Omniterra Media Inc
First Edition
Visit the author's website at www.rexmorton.com
For information regarding special discounts for bulk purchases, please contact Rex Morton Publishing Special Sales at rex@rexmorton.com.

Disclaimer

This book is intended to provide information about the fields of Neuro-Linguistic Programming (NLP) and Cognitive Behavioural Therapy (CBT) and their potential integration. While the author has made every effort to ensure that the information was correct at the time of publication, the author does not assume and hereby disclaims any liability to any party for any loss, damage, or disruption caused by errors or omissions, whether such errors or omissions result from negligence, accident, or any other cause.

The contents of this book should not be used as a substitute for professional advice, diagnosis, or treatment. The reader should always consult a qualified healthcare provider about mental health concerns or conditions. Never disregard professional psychological or medical advice or delay in seeking it because of something you have read in this book.

The views expressed in this work are solely those of the author and do not necessarily reflect the views of the publisher, and the publisher hereby disclaims any responsibility for them.

Including websites, links, or references to other resources does not mean that the author or the publisher endorses the

1.1 Defining Neuro-Linguistic Programming

Neuro-Linguistic Programming, popularly known as NLP, is a unique approach to communication, personal development, and psychotherapy. The name itself offers a hint to its scope: "neuro" refers to the brain and neural network that feed into our five senses; "linguistic" relates to the insights language bestows about our thinking; and "programming" signifies how we can choose to think and feel, much like programming a computer.

NLP focuses on the fundamental dynamics between the brainand language and how their interaction influences our body and behavior (programming). It provides a conceptual framework and a set of instruments for understanding how the human mind functions and how to harness its potential for personal development and change.

1.2 History and Evolution of NLP

The concept of Neuro-Linguistic Programming was developed in the 1970s by Richard Bandler, a mathematician and information scientist, and John Grinder, a linguist. Initially, Bandler and Grinder were intrigued by the powerful change work performed by therapists like Virginia Satir (a family therapist), Fritz Perls (the developer of Gestalt Therapy), and Milton H. Erickson (a pioneering hypnotherapist). They observed these therapists and came up with a model of how they communicated with patients, aiming to replicate their techniques and produce the same impressive results.

In the following years, the scope of NLP expanded considerably, transcending the initial therapeutic context. It has been utilized in fields as varied as business, education, sports, negotiation, and, as will be explored later in this book, mental health.

1.3 The Key Principles of NLP

The effectiveness of NLP is grounded in several key principles:

The Map is Not the Territory: This principle emphasizes that our perception of reality is not reality itself but rather our own internalized subjective experience of it. We all have different mental maps of the world, formed by our experiences, beliefs, values, and assumptions.

Experience has a Structure: Our thoughts and behaviours are not random but follow patterns. By understanding these patterns, we can alter them to change undesired behaviours or responses.

If One Person Can Do Something, Anyone Can Learn to Do It: This principle suggests that we can model the skills of others and acquire them ourselves.

Mind and Body are Part of the Same System: This principle recognizes the interconnectedness of our mental and physical selves. Changes in one component can influence the other.

The Positive Intention Behind Every Behaviour: NLP assumes that all behaviour serves or once served a positive intention, even if the outcome is negative. This understanding allows for greater empathy and better communication.

Choice is Better than No Choice: Having more options provides greater freedom and flexibility, enabling us to respond more effectively to a variety of situations.

Understanding and integrating these principles is foundational to successfully utilizing NLP techniques, whether to enhance communication, foster personal development, or tackle mental health issues like anxiety and depression, which we will explore in the upcoming chapters.

2.1 The Nature and Impact of Anxiety and Depression

Anxiety and depression are two of the most prevalent mental health disorders that affect millions of people worldwide. They are not just simple feelings of sadness or worry, but complex emotional states that can have a profound impact on a person's quality of life.

Anxiety disorders are characterized by excessive and persistent worry about everyday situations. These feelings are often disproportionate to the actual event and can interfere with daily activities. Anxiety can manifest in several forms, including Generalized Anxiety Disorder (GAD), Panic Disorder, Social Anxiety Disorder, and various phobia-related disorders.

Depression, on the other hand, is more than simply feeling melancholy or experiencing a difficult time. It is a severe mental illness that affects how you feel, think, and function on a daily basis. Depression may manifest as persistent sadness, loss of interest in once-enjoyed activities, changes in appetite or weight, difficulty resting or oversleeping, and, in severe cases, suicidal or death-related thoughts.

Both of these conditions can severely impact an individual's ability to function and enjoy life. They can strain relationships, decrease productivity at work, and contribute to various physical health problems over time.

2.2 Current Treatment Approaches

Treating anxiety and depression often involves a combination of psychotherapy (talk therapy), medication, and lifestyle changes.

Psychotherapy, such as cognitive-behavioural therapy (CBT) and interpersonal therapy (IPT), can help individuals understand and manage their condition. These therapies aim to change negative thinking patterns and improve coping skills, thus reducing symptoms.

Medication is frequently used to treat anxiety and depression. Included among these are selective serotonin reuptake inhibitors (SSRIs), serotonin and norepinephrine reuptake inhibitors (SNRIs), benzodiazepines, and others. Notably, these medications should be prescribed and managed by a medical professional, as they may cause adverse effects and withdrawal symptoms.

Lifestyle changes, such as regular exercise, a healthy diet, adequate sleep, and reduced alcohol and caffeine, can also help manage symptoms and improve overall well-being.

2.3 The Mind-Body Connection in Mental Health

The mind and body are not separate entities; they are deeply interconnected. The mind can influence the body's functioning, just as physical conditions can impact mental health. This bi-directional relationship is especially evident in the context of anxiety and depression.

For instance, chronic stress and anxiety can cause a variety of physical symptoms, including migraines, muscle tension, insomnia, and digestive issues. Depression can manifest physiologically in a variety of ways, including changes in appetite and sleep patterns. Conversely, chronic physical ailments such as diabetes and cardiovascular disease can also increase the risk of mental health disorders.

This understanding of the mind-body connection underscores the importance of holistic approaches to mental health treatment. In the next chapter, we'll delve into the science behind Neuro-Linguistic Programming (NLP) and how it leverages this connection to treat conditions like anxiety and depression.

3.1 The Intersection of Neuroscience and Linguistics

Neuro-Linguistic Programming (NLP) sits at the crossroads of neuroscience and linguistics. It uses the insights from both fields to create techniques for positive personal change.

From the perspective of neuroscience, our thoughts, behaviours, and emotions are all rooted in the neurological processes happening within our brain. These processes, in turn, are shaped by the stimuli we encounter and our responses to them.

Linguistics, on the other hand, explores how language structures our thoughts and influences our perception of reality. The words we use to describe our experiences don't just reflect our reality – they help to shape it.

By combining these insights, NLP creates a unique model of human experience. It acknowledges that our internal representation of the world, created by our neurology and shaped by our language, influences how we think, feel, and act.

By changing this internal representation, we can change our experiences.

3.2 Understanding the Brain's Plasticity

One of the key principles of neuroscience that underpins NLP is the concept of neuroplasticity – the brain's ability to change and adapt in response to new experiences, learning, and injury.

For a long time, it was believed that the brain was a static organ that, once fully developed, could not change. However, advances in neuroscience have demonstrated that the brain is incredibly dynamic, continually remodeling itself based on our experiences.

This plasticity is what allows us to learn new skills, form memories, and adapt to new situations. It also means that we have the potential to change negative thought patterns, beliefs, or behaviours that may contribute to mental health conditions like anxiety and depression.

3.3 How Neuro-Linguistic Programming Modulates Thought Patterns

NLP techniques are designed to leverage the brain's plasticity to change our internal representations of the world and, consequently, our responses to it.

For example, one common technique used in NLP is known as "reframing". This involves changing the way we perceive a particular situation or experience, thereby changing our emotional response to it. By consciously reframing our thoughts, we can change our neurological responses and, consequently, our emotions and behaviours.

Similarly, techniques like "anchoring" allow us to create a neurological link between a specific stimulus and a desired emotional state. This "anchor" can then be used to quickly and easily access this desired state whenever needed.

In essence, NLP offers a range of tools and techniques to consciously influence our brain's wiring. By doing so, we can bring about positive changes in our mental health and overall well-being. In the following chapters, we'll delve into how these tools can be used specifically to tackle anxiety and depression.

4.1 Introduction to the Neuro-Linguistic Programming Communication Model

The Neuro-Linguistic Programming (NLP) communication model describes how our minds filter information from the outside world. It reveals how we interpret our experiences and how these interpretations influence our responses.

This model suggests that we take in information from the world around us through our five senses (visual, auditory, kinesthetic, olfactory, and gustatory). This raw data is then processed through various mental filters (such as our beliefs, values, memories, decisions, and language), creating our internal representations of the world.

These internal representations influence our state (mood or feeling) and physiology (bodily responses), which in turn affect our behaviours. Through this process, the NLP communication model illustrates how our perceptions shape our reality and responses.

4.2 How Mental Health Conditions Distort Communication

In the context of mental health conditions like anxiety and depression, this process of communication can become distorted. Negative beliefs and assumptions can create unhelpful mental filters, leading to distorted internal representations of reality.

For example, an individual with anxiety may have a mental filter that magnifies potential threats and downplays their ability to cope, leading to feelings of intense worry and physical symptoms like a racing heart. Similarly, someone with depression may have a mental filter that highlights negative experiences and diminishes positive ones, leading to feelings of sadness and hopelessness.

These distortions in internal representation can perpetuate the mental health condition, creating a vicious cycle of negative thoughts, feelings, and behaviours.

4.3 The Role of the Neuro-Linguistic Programming Communication Model in Mental Health Restoration

The NLP communication model provides a useful framework for understanding and addressing these distortions in internal representation. By identifying and modifying the unhelpful mental filters, it is possible to change the internal representations and, consequently, the resulting emotional states and behaviours.

NLP offers a range of techniques to achieve this, including 'reframing', 'submodalities', 'anchoring', and 'parts integration', among others. These techniques help individuals change their thought patterns, challenge unhelpful beliefs, and develop new, more helpful responses to their experiences.

For instance, 'reframing' can help an individual with anxiety to view a perceived threat as a challenge to be overcome rather than something to be feared. This change in perception can reduce feelings of worry and increase feelings of confidence and control.

In essence, the NLP communication model offers a practical and effective approach to mental health restoration. By targeting the root cause of the issue – the distortions in internal representation – it provides a pathway for individuals to regain control over their thoughts, feelings, and behaviours.

5.1 Visualization and Anchoring Techniques

One powerful way that Neuro-Linguistic Programming (NLP) addresses anxiety is through the use of visualization and anchoring techniques. These techniques help individuals replace feelings of anxiety with more positive and empowering states.

Visualization involves creating a mental image of a desired outcome or state. For instance, one might visualize oneself confidently delivering a presentation at work, or calmly facing a fear-inducing situation. Visualization is believed to 'prime' the brain to respond in a desired manner when the actual situation occurs.

Anchoring involves associating this desired state with a specific cue or 'anchor', such as a unique touch, a specific word, or a unique visual cue. This anchor can then be used to quickly trigger the desired state in real-life situations. For example, one might anchor the feeling of calm and confidence to the act of tapping a finger against the thumb, and then use this anchor to access this state whenever feelings of anxiety start to emerge.

5.2 Swish Pattern Technique

The Swish Pattern is another NLP technique that can be particularly effective for tackling anxiety. This technique involves replacing an undesired response (in this case, feelings of anxiety) with a more desired one.

The process involves visualizing a situation that triggers anxiety and then 'swishing' this image away and replacing it with a visual representation of oneself confidently handling the situation. With repeated practice, the brain learns to associate the anxiety-inducing situation with the confident response rather than the anxious one. This can help reduce feelings of anxiety and improve responses to anxiety-provoking situations.

5.3 Submodalities for Anxiety Management

Submodalities are the finer distinctions or the 'sub-qualities' of our sensory representations. For example, in the visual realm, submodalities can include aspects like color, brightness, distance, and size.

Changing these submodalities can change the way we experience our internal representations, and consequently, our emotional responses. For instance, if one has a mental image that provokes anxiety, changing its submodalities (like reducing its size, moving it further away, or making it black and white) can reduce its emotional impact.

Similarly, enhancing the submodalities of a positive, empowering image (like making it bigger, brighter, or closer) can increase its emotional impact, making it easier to access positive states.

In essence, these NLP techniques offer effective tools to reprogram our brain's responses to anxiety-provoking situations. By changing our internal representations and the emotional states associated with them, we can change our behaviours and improve our overall well-being.

6.1 Time-Line Therapy

Time-Line Therapy is a powerful NLP technique that can be especially effective for treating depression. Depression often involves a negative outlook on the past, present, and future, and Time-Line Therapy can help modify these perceptions.

This technique involves visualizing one's 'time line' – the imaginary line that represents your past, present, and future. By 'traveling' along this time line, individuals can revisit past experiences, modify their perceptions of these experiences, and imagine a more positive future.

For instance, they can reframe past experiences that contribute to feelings of worthlessness or guilt, two common symptoms of depression. They can also create a more empowering vision of their future, which can instill hope and motivation – emotions that are often lacking in depression.

6.2 The Disney Strategy

The Disney Strategy is an NLP technique based on the creative process used by Walt Disney. It involves three stages – the dreamer, the realist, and the critic – each of which represents a different thinking style.

Depression often involves a predominance of the critic style – a focus on what's wrong, what's not working, or why things won't work. The Disney Strategy aims to balance this by fostering the dreamer and the realist thinking styles.

The dreamer stage encourages individuals to visualize a future where they are free from depression, while the realist stage helps them identify practical steps to achieve this future. The critic stage is then used constructively to identify potential obstacles and ways to overcome them.

6.3 Parts Integration Technique

Depression often involves internal conflicts, like wanting to change but feeling incapable of doing so. The Parts Integration Technique can help resolve these conflicts.

This technique involves identifying the different 'parts' or aspects of the self that are in conflict and facilitating a dialogue between them. The aim is to understand the positive intentions of each part and find a way for them to work together.

For example, one part might want to socialize more to improve mood, while another part might fear the vulnerability involved in social interaction. Through a guided dialogue, these parts can understand each other's intentions, find common ground, and work together to create a more balanced social life.

By combining these NLP techniques, individuals can address the root causes of their depression, change their thought patterns, and create a more positive and empowering outlook on life.

7.1 Steps for Self-applying NLP Techniques

Applying NLP techniques by oneself can be a powerful way to manage anxiety and depression. Here are the basic steps to self-applying these techniques:

Identify the Issue: Begin by identifying the specific issue you want to address. For example, you might want to reduce feelings of anxiety associated with public speaking or challenge beliefs of worthlessness that contribute to depression.

Choose an Appropriate NLP Technique: Next, choose an NLP technique that seems best suited to your issue. For instance, if you're dealing with anxiety related to public speaking, you might choose to use the anchoring technique to associate feelings of confidence with the act of speaking in public.

Apply the Technique: Now, apply the chosen technique. Using the anchoring example, you could first visualize yourself speaking confidently in public. Once you're fully immersed in this visualization and can feel the associated confidence, set your anchor (for example, pressing your thumb and index finger together).

Practice Regularly: Finally, practice regularly. The more frequently you use your anchor (or apply whatever technique you've chosen), the stronger the association will become. Over time, you'll find that simply activating your anchor can help you feel more confident when public speaking.

Example: Let's say you are dealing with depressive thoughts stemming from a belief of being unlovable. You can use the Reframing technique for this issue. Start by identifying the thought or belief you want to reframe (e.g., "I am unlovable"). Then, try to see this belief from a different perspective or context that diminishes its negative impact or even turns it into a positive statement (e.g., "Not everyone will love me, and that's okay. This allows me to appreciate the love I do receive more deeply").

7.2 Precautions and Limitations of Self-application

While self-applying NLP techniques can be effective, it's essential to be aware of certain precautions and limitations:

Understand the Technique Well: Before applying any NLP technique, make sure you understand it well. Misapplying these techniques can lead to ineffective results or even unintended negative effects.

Not a Replacement for Professional Help: NLP techniques can be a useful tool for managing symptoms of anxiety and depression, but they're not a replacement for professional help. If your symptoms are severe, persistent, or causing significant distress, seek help from a mental health professional.

Individual Differences: Everyone is different, and what works for one person might not work for another. If a particular technique doesn't seem to be helping, don't get discouraged. Try a different technique or approach, and remember that it's okay to ask for help if you need it.

Patience and Consistency: Changing thought patterns and behaviours takes time and consistent effort. Don't expect immediate results, and don't be too hard on yourself if progress is slow. Keep practicing, and celebrate small victories along the way.

By keeping these steps and precautions in mind, self-application of NLP techniques can become a valuable tool in your mental health toolkit.

8.1 How Neuro-Linguistic Programming Therapies Work

Professional Neuro-Linguistic Programming (NLP) therapies involve working with a certified NLP practitioner to overcome mental health challenges like anxiety and depression. These sessions usually involve one-on-one counseling, but they can also be conducted in group settings.

In a typical NLP therapy session, the practitioner will start by discussing your issues and goals. They will then apply various NLP techniques tailored to your specific needs. These techniques aim to change unhelpful thought patterns and behaviours and replace them with more constructive ones.

For example, if you are dealing with anxiety related to a traumatic experience, an NLP practitioner might use the 'Change History' technique. This process involves revisiting the traumatic event and changing your perception of it, thereby reducing its impact on your current state.

In case of depression related to feelings of worthlessness, the practitioner might use the 'Belief Change' technique. This process involves identifying and challenging the belief causing distress, then replacing it with a more positive and empowering belief.

NLP therapy can be highly personalized, with the practitioner adjusting the techniques based on your responses and progress.

8.2 Choosing the Right Neuro-Linguistic Programming Practitioner

Choosing the right NLP practitioner is a crucial step in your therapeutic journey. Here are a few factors to consider:

Certification and Training: Ensure that the practitioner is certified and has received proper training in NLP. Different levels of certification (such as Practitioner, Master Practitioner, and Trainer) reflect different levels of expertise.

Experience: Look for a practitioner with experience in treating your specific issue (anxiety or depression in this case). They should be able to demonstrate a history of success in helping clients with similar challenges.

Approach and Personality: NLP therapy is a collaborative process, so it's essential to find a practitioner with whom you feel comfortable. You should feel heard, understood, and respected in their presence.

Professional Ethics: The practitioner should uphold professional ethics, including maintaining confidentiality, respecting boundaries, and providing safe and supportive care.

Client Testimonials and Reviews: Check for client testimonials and reviews to gauge the practitioner's effectiveness and professionalism.

Remember, professional NLP therapies can be an invaluable tool in overcoming anxiety and depression, but they should be viewed as part of a comprehensive mental health treatment plan that might also include medication, other forms of therapy, and lifestyle modifications. Always consult with a healthcare provider or mental health professional when making decisions about your treatment.

9.1 The Strengths of Neuro-Linguistic Programming in Mental Health Care

Neuro-Linguistic Programming (NLP) has several strengths in mental health care. Firstly, NLP is highly flexible and customizable to an individual's specific needs. Techniques can be adapted and applied in various ways to suit different individuals and issues.

Secondly, NLP focuses on the 'here and now' and is often goal-oriented, making it practical and actionable. Rather than delving into past traumas, NLP emphasizes changing current perceptions and behaviours to achieve desired outcomes.

Thirdly, NLP equips individuals with tools they can use independently to manage their mental health. Techniques like visualization, anchoring, and reframing can be practiced independently, giving individuals a greater sense of control over their mental health.

9.2 The Limitations and Criticisms of Neuro-Linguistic Programming

Despite its strengths, NLP has also been met with some criticism. One of the main criticisms is the lack of rigorous scientific evidence supporting its efficacy. While many individuals report positive experiences with NLP, there are fewer scientifically controlled studies that definitively establish its effectiveness.

Additionally, the quality of NLP therapy can vary greatly depending on the practitioner. Since NLP lacks a unified governing body or standard certification process, the level of expertise and ethical conduct among practitioners can vary. This means that the effectiveness of NLP therapy often depends heavily on the specific practitioner.

9.3 Evaluating the Evidence: Does Neuro-Linguistic Programming Really Work for Anxiety and Depression?

The evidence for NLP's effectiveness in treating anxiety and depression is mixed. While many individual case reports and small-scale studies report positive results, larger and more rigorous scientific studies are relatively fewer.

Some research has suggested that NLP techniques can help reduce symptoms of anxiety and depression and improve overall wellbeing. However, other studies have found no significant difference between NLP and other forms of therapy, or have called for more high-quality research to be conducted.

while NLP may be beneficial for many individuals, its effectiveness is not yet definitively established in the scientific literature. As with any therapeutic approach, what works best will depend on the individual. Always consult with a healthcare provider or mental health professional when making decisions about your treatment.

10.1 Emerging Trends in Neuro-Linguistic Programming for Mental Health

As we move into the future, we can expect to see some exciting developments in the application of Neuro-Linguistic Programming (NLP) for mental health. One emerging trend is the integration of NLP with technology. This might involve the development of NLP-based apps or virtual reality experiences to help individuals manage their anxiety and depression.

Another potential trend is the increasing emphasis on evidence-based practice in NLP. This involves conducting more rigorous scientific research to determine the effectiveness of different NLP techniques and to refine these techniques based on the research findings.

10.2 Integrating Neuro-Linguistic Programming with Other Therapeutic Approaches

One promising direction for the future of NLP in mental health treatment is its integration with other therapeutic approaches. For instance, NLP techniques could be integrated with Cognitive-

Behavioural Therapy (CBT) to create a more comprehensive treatment plan.

CBT, which focuses on identifying and challenging negative thought patterns, could be complemented by NLP techniques that aim to change these thought patterns at a deeper, subconscious level. Alternatively, NLP could be used alongside mindfulness-based therapies to increase present-moment awareness and reduce negative rumination.

10.3 Final Thoughts on Neuro-Linguistic Programming's Role in Mental Health

While the role of NLP in treating anxiety and depression is still being explored and understood, it undeniably offers valuable tools for enhancing mental health and well-being. Its emphasis on personal growth, positive thinking, and self-empowerment aligns well with a holistic approach to mental health care.

However, as we move forward, it is vital to ensure that NLP practice is grounded in scientific evidence and that it is practiced ethically and professionally. Additionally, we must remember that NLP, like any therapeutic approach, may not work for everyone or for every issue. It should therefore be viewed as one tool among many in the mental health toolkit.

With ongoing research, open dialogue, and careful practice, the future of NLP in overcoming anxiety and depression looks promising. As with any approach to mental health care, the ultimate goal is to help individuals lead happier, healthier, and more fulfilling lives.

Rex Morton is a renowned author and researcher in the United Kingdom with a passionate interest in the human mind, specifically in Cognitive Behavioural Therapy (CBT) and Neuro-Linguistic Programming (NLP).

Morton has spent a considerable portion of his professional life diving deep into the theories and principles that form the backbone of these two compelling fields.

Although Morton does not have clinical experience, his intense curiosity and dedication to studying these subjects have made him a respected figure in the field. He has thoroughly researched the integration of NLP techniques into CBT, offering fresh perspectives and insights into how these two methodologies can complement each other to enhance understanding of human cognition and behaviour.

As an author, Morton has successfully communicated his knowledge and passion to a broader audience, making complex psychological theories accessible to professionals and interested laypersons. His writing is characterized by a clear, engaging style and a focus on the practical application of theories, making them relevant to everyday life.

In his personal life, Morton is an ardent lover of the natural world, often spending his free time exploring the British countryside. His passion for landscape photography allows him to capture and share the beauty of these excursions. Despite his accomplishments, Morton is known for his humility and eagerness to continue learning. His work continues to inspire those interested in the intricate workings of the human mind and the exciting possibilities presented by the integration of NLP and CBT.

If you've found the content of this book enlightening and wish to continue your journey of understanding the human mind, I warmly invite you to visit my website at www.rexmorton.com. The website serves as a hub of knowledge where I share my latest findings, thoughts, and insights on NLP and related topics.

I also encourage you to subscribe to the newsletter available on the website. By subscribing, you'll receive regular updates on a range of topics, from detailed discussions on specific NLP techniques and their application in other fields to the latest research.

The newsletter is also the first place I'll share news of upcoming releases. Whether it's the announcement of a new book, the launch of an online course, newsletter subscribers will be the first to know. This is a great opportunity to continue learning directly from me, deepening your understanding of NLP and related topics, and enhancing your skills in applying these techniques in your own life or professional practice.
I'm looking forward to sharing this journey with you.